Philip Bennett Power

The Oiled Feather

Philip Bennett Power

The Oiled Feather

ISBN/EAN: 9783743327146

Manufactured in Europe, USA, Canada, Australia, Japa

Cover: Foto ©ninafisch / pixelio.de

Manufactured and distributed by brebook publishing software
(www.brebook.com)

Philip Bennett Power

The Oiled Feather

THE

OILED FEATHER

Illustrated.

BY THE

REV. P. B. POWER, M.A.,

LATE INCUMBENT OF CHRIST CHURCH, WORTHING.

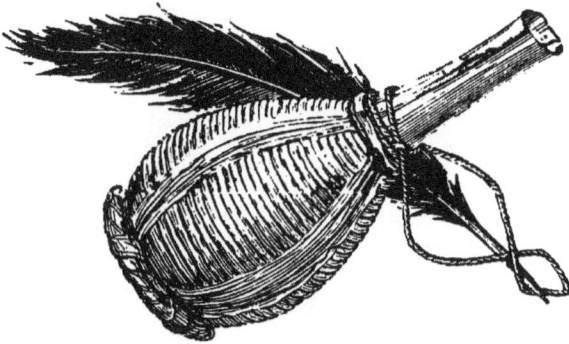

LONDON:

HAMILTON, ADAMS, AND CO.

MDCCCLXXI.

To the Reader.

ALL male and female Joes here see,
How tempers sour bring misery;
What's soft and kind, and sweet and tender,
Suits male and female,—either gender.
"You shall!" "I say!" "Come now!" "You
    must!"
Is just so much corroding rust.
Love is the secret,—love, the oil
To keep hearts bright, nor let them spoil.
Wife, husband oil,—and husband, wife,
And you shall lead a happy life.
The cross, the rude, the hard, the fickle,
Cannot resist this feather's tickle;
The oil that's on it is so sly,
One drop is oft enough to try.
You need not use enough to smother,
But just enough to please each other.
The way to meet life's rusting weather,
Is just to use a well "Oiled Feather!"

Chapter First.

IN THE VILLAGE of Hurst lived two neighbours named Joseph Irons and Samuel Parsons. Joseph Irons went by the name of "Rusty Joe," and Samuel Parsons by that of "Polished Sam." The names were characteristic of the men, Joseph Irons being a short tart kind of man in his dealings with his fellow-creatures; and Samuel Parsons being on the other hand genial and civil. Joseph Irons wouldn't put his hand to his hat for any man, not he! he

wouldn't waste his time with palavering
people with fine words, no, not he! if folk
didn't like his goods, they may leave them;
and if they didn't like his answers, they
needn't ask him any questions; in a word,
"Rusty Joe," though very honest, and very
decent living, was disliked by almost everybody; and, in truth, no one could be
surprised.

On the other hand, Samuel Parsons was
a general favourite; he had a salute for
every one who came in the way; he didn't
think himself a bit the worse man, because
he put his hand to his hat to the parson
and the squire, as well as bobbed his head
to the old apple-woman at the corner of
the street. As to civil words, Sam's theory
was that, they were quite as little trouble
to speak as gruff ones; and they certainly
slipped more pleasant-like out of one's
mouth; and so it came to pass, that go
wherever you would, all the country round,
amongst all sorts and conditions of men,

everybody liked Sam Parsons, and we may
wind up this paragraph, just as we did the
last, by saying, and in truth, no one could
be surprised.

" Polished Sam " and " Rusty Joe "
might have lived on to the end of the
world, for aught that we have to do with

them, were it not that they afford us some very useful lessons, which will teach us, if we learn them, how to avoid a great deal of unpleasantness, in this rusty crusty world of ours. The world is full of Rusty Joes, and Rusty Joes' wives too; and folk make no small part of their own misery, by bumping and thumping against one another, when the road is wide enough for all; and by being grumpy and growly when a wee bit of civility would answer the purpose quite as well. Folk should remember the great mechanical law that "action and re-action are equal and contrary;" that is, put into plain words; if you throw a ball against a wall, the wall will hit the ball, as hard as the ball hits the wall, only in an opposite direction; or if you like to put it into the language of daily life, it will read thus, "If you thump me, I'll thump you; and moreover I'll thump you as hard as you thump me." Of course we consider this an un-Christian way of

going through life; all we say is that, it
is a very common one.

Well, we shall see how "Rusty Joe"
and "Polished Sam" got through one day
of their existence; one day will be quite
enough for such a little book as this.

"Come, bring the oil flask, there's a
pet," said Samuel Parsons to his wife, as
he finished screwing a new lock on his
front door. Sam, of course, needn't have
said, "there's a pet," unless he liked; but
he used to think it was a great shame that
women were called all sorts of pretty
names before they were married, but none
afterwards. "I say," says Sam, "many of
the poor creatures are cheated with them
there pretty names; poor folk! they think
they'll always get them; but they become
mighty scarce after they finger the ring."
We don't mean to tell all the names Sam
called his wife, before they were married;
but now he called her "pet;" and as soon
as she heard the loving word, she threw

down her duster on the chair, and sped
off to the kitchen for the flask. The flask
had a feather in it, as such flasks generally
have; and Sam, taking the said feather
between his forefinger and thumb, oiled
the key of the street door right well, and
then locked it and unlocked it a dozen
times; at first it went stiff, and required
some strength of wrist to turn it; but as
it was worked to and fro, and the oil
began to make its way into the wards, it
worked more and more easily; until at last,
Tommy, Sam's little son, who was standing
by, was able to turn it almost with a
touch; and then, Sam pronounced that it
would do.

This operation finished, Sam thought he'd
just give his knife a touch of the end of
the feather; less than a drop out of the
flask would do; just a mere touch, that
was all it wanted; and presently, to young
Tommy's great delight, his father made the
blade go up and down, click, click. Tommy

evidently approved of the result, for he began to click, click with his tongue and the roof of his mouth in imitation; and how long he might have delayed his father we can't tell; if it were not that Mrs. Parsons caught him up in her arms, and made off with him; she calling Tommy a "saucy rogue" and kissing him all the way; and he on his part "click, clicking," as though his mouth were a cutler's shop, and you were opening and shutting every knife in it.

Some folk might think that Sam Parsons had done enough in the oiling line for one day; but there was one thing more to do, and then he would be quite ready to take his potatoes to market. One or two of the wheels of his waggon had been a trifle creaky, so he took the grease pot, and just gave them a touch of its contents; you could have rolled all he put upon them into the size of a couple of marbles, but 'twas quite enough; the wheels gave over creaking; and if the old proverb be true, that "Silence gives consent!" no doubt, they highly approved of what Sam had done.

"Now, then, I'm off to market," said Sam. "Good bye, Jenny, pet." Oh that little word, "pet;" didn't the cunning fellow oil his wife's temper, and even almost her very joints, for her day's work, when he called her that little name! "Good bye, Tommy, my darling." Oh you cunning man! there you are with your oiled feather again; for when Tommy was naughty, and his mother reminded him that she must tell his father, when he came home, and "father would be sore grieved if his darling was naughty," wasn't Tommy good; for child though he was, he was able to reason thus much in his mind: Tommy is father's darling, and he won't vex him; darlings ought not to vex those who love them. Never mind, good reader, if there's a flaw in the logic; nursery logic is sometimes very funny reasoning, but it answered the purpose; naughty Tommy became good, and clicked, clicked about the house as merry as a sunbeam, instead of sprawling and bawling on the ground; and all because his father happened to call him a " darling " before he went out.

Is it any wonder that thus, like loving American beetles, pulling together at their load instead of kicking at each other, Sam

B

Parsons and his wife rolled little Sam famously along, even though sometimes, owing to diverse causes, it was pretty stiff work.

"I say, Polly," said Sam Parsons to his one servant-maid, as he left the house, "don't forget to clean up those irons, if you can manage it, there's a good lass: you'll find the oil flask hanging up behind the kitchen door;" and so, with a cheerful smile on his countenance, Sam Parsons took his departure for market. Ah! cunning Sam; before he went, he oiled his wife and child, and now he oiled the servant maid; and when he turned his back upon his own door, he left smiling faces and glad hearts behind him; and I warrant he found them all smiling to receive him when he came home.

Chapter Second.

"RUSTY JOE" shall have a chapter to himself, we won't mix him up with "Polished Sam" on any account; acid and sweet make a very good drink when mixed together; and we dare say Joe and Sam must meet before our story's done; and if they do, we hope it will be to do the reader good; but they must keep asunder for awhile.

"Rusty Joe" had an idea that, it was rather letting one's self down to be civil; he could not see the distinction between being sneaking, and cringing, and time-serving, in one's conduct, and being civil and pleasant; he prided himself on being blunt, and honest, and upright, aye, and downright too; but he forgot that he was often rude, and surly, and morose.

Now, on this very morning, "Rusty Joe" was going to market also! and it so happened that, he ought to have done what his neighbour "Polished Sam" had done; but he was above attending to such little things; and provided a thing could be done at all, he did not mind if it were by main force; a pull and a bang would do as well as anything else; but pulls and bangs knock one's temper about a great deal; this, however, "Rusty Joe" did not take into account.

Before it was time for Joseph Irons to leave his house on this eventful day, he had as much misery as would fall to his neighbour "Polished Sam" in a year. In the first place, he had neglected to grease his boots after last market day, which had been very wet; and now, when he went to put on these same boots, (for the day promised to be wet again,) they were so hard and stiff that he pulled, and kicked, and knocked, and stamped in vain. A very little of this work will try a man's temper, and at last Joe was about to give up in despair, when with a final pull and

kick he knocked one foot into a boot;
and seeing that it would be almost as hard
to pull out the leg, once it was in, as to
get in the other, he knocked and kicked
away, until the second got in also. Bad
temper is always bad for a man's digestion,
and sometimes it will make him quarrel

even with his meat; hence, we need not be surprised to hear that nothing was right that morning at breakfast. The eggs were too hard, and the bread was too soft; the bacon dish was too . hot, and the tea-pot was too cold; and who can wonder, when Joe's two boots, as hard and stiff as if they had been frozen, were pinching his toes and heels, just as if they had ten wicked fingers, with ten long claws on them. Ah ! Joseph Irons, you should have greased your boots, or put the least· drop in the world of linseed oil upon them, and you would have agreed much better with your breakfast; aye, and your breakfast would have agreed much better with you.

When·Joseph Irons had bolted his break-fast, he got up, and went to the street door to go out; but no loving word did he speak to his wife Betty, who, if the truth were known, was by no means sorry to get rid of him and his tempers, for awhile. True ! Joseph never abused his wife; but he was exacting, and unsympa-thizing, and gave very few kind words; and the consequence was, she just creaked along through life's duties. She did not run smoothly and swiftly, like the wheels of Sam Parsons' waggon; nor had she any spring in her, like his well oiled penknife; nor did she move about comfortably through the ins and outs of life, as Sam Parsons's oiled key did through the wards of his lock; she was a poor downhearted creature, who never basked in the sunshine of a little love; who never heard the music of an affectionate word; who had indeed all the machinery of a woman's heart, with all its great capacity for doing wondrous things; but there was just something wanted to set it all a-going—it was a little love.

"Mind you have my shirt finished to-night," said Joe Irons, as he laid his hand on the street door, "for I may have to go to Pitbank to-morrow, and

I don't want to go to the Squire's in
this old concern;" and with this direction to his wife, Mr. Irons took himself
off.

But if Joe Irons met with trouble from
want of a little oil, even before he got
to his street door, he met with more when
he got to the door itself. The door was
stiff in its hinges, and stiff in the lock;
aye, as stiff, as if it had had the rheumatics
for twenty years. After a little difficulty
Joe Irons opened his door, but he could
not shut it with as little trouble again.
That door seemed to have a will of its
own; and unfortunately, it was not just
now the same as Joe Irons' will—perhaps
it might have thought that the house,
which smelt a little fusty, might be the
better for some ventilation; or, may be,
it was simply obstinate and wouldn't shut;
but so it was that, Joe gave it five or six
pulls without success. Now, it was no new
thing to Joseph Irons to pull that door;

he despised such a small thing as a drop of oil; the door had hitherto yielded to main force, and his strength was in no wise abated; so, "here goes," said he, and he gave it a bang with all his might. There was no resisting such an appeal as this; so the door was shut with a bang loud enough to rouse the whole neighbourhood; but, alas; my poor friend, Joe, you don't know what harm you did; you actually shook the house, and broke a glass shade upon the chimney piece in the parlor. That glass shade was part of the only ornament in the room; it covered two or three foreign birds, which Mrs. Irons' brother, who had been a mate in a vessel, brought her home from foreign parts; and Mrs. Irons was very much vexed. Had her husband spoken a kind word or two to her before leaving, she would in all probability have put up with the loss for his sake; but he had done nothing of the kind; and the consequence was, when the glass came tumbling down, she felt very irritated and sore.

This, then, was the way that "Rusty Joe" started forth to market; he met with trouble before he went to his street door; and when he arrived at it; and as we shall presently see, with plenty more before he returned to it again.

The market town of Stoke was full ten miles from the village where "Rusty Joe" and "Polished Sam" lived; and there was a good deal of up-hill road on the way thither. The road was moreover heavy, for recent rain had fallen, and there seemed to be a prospect of more. Already had "Rusty Joe" lost some time over his boots, and over the door; and it behoved him now to make as much speed as he could, in order to reach the market at all in time; of this he was well aware, so he smacked his whip frequently as he cleared the bounds of the village, and got out into the open road. But Joe's troubles still lay thick before him; he soon found himself a poor limping creature, and every step he took seemed to have a corresponding pinch belonging to it. Presently, he began to feel conscious that he must be late for market, unless he could get on a little faster; and accordingly, at any hazard to his unfortunate ten toes, he smacked his whip, and jee-hupped to his horses; but he soon found that they could not make much more way than himself. What was the matter? Was the load heavier than usual? Were the roads heavier? No, but "Rusty Joe" had not greased the wheels of his waggon for a long time; and now the vehicle went on, creak, creak, as though it would come to pieces every moment. Main force was Joe's resource on all occasions, so he whipped the horses, and they pulled with all their might; but at the Blackford hill, they found the waggon so hard to move, that they had to stop over and over again.

Instead of making allowances for the poor beasts, which were really doing their best, our friend "Rusty Joe" determined to make them drag the waggon up the hill; accordingly, he pulled a piece of whipcord out of his pocket, and his knife also; and while the horses stood puffing, and panting, and blowing, with their exertions, he prepared to fit on a new lash. "I'll tickle you, my lads," said "Rusty Joe," and so saying, he applied his thumb nail to the knife, to open the blade to cut the cord. The knife was stiff; in fact, the hinge of the blade was rusted; but the angry man would not lose any time over it: he'd *make* it open in a jiffey; force, with him, would do everything; and with a tremendous effort, he half opened the blade; but in doing so, he tore his nail down to the quick; and the pain soon made itself plainly felt. Still the angry man was not to be put off; he cut the whipcord; he put on a new lash; and with a crack, crack, crack, he tried to start the horses with the creaking waggon up hill; but force will not do everything in the world; the horses made such a plunge, under the influence of the smarting lash, that the harness broke, and there stood "Rusty Joe" in a sad plight, neither able to go on nor to return.

Joe! you should have greased your boots, and you would not have been late.

Joe! you should have oiled your door, and you would not have lost your temper.

Joe! you should have oiled your waggon wheels, and then your horses could have pulled it up the hill.

Joe! you should have oiled your pen-knife, and you would not have torn your nail.

Joe! you should have oiled your harness; and the leather would not have become rotten, and broken, as it has now done, in your time of need.

Now we must leave you there, Joe, upon

the roadside, to meditate upon these things for awhile. There Joe sat, as prickly as the teazle which grew in the hedge road at his side, ready to stick into any body or anything that came near him. Poor fellow! we are sorry, no doubt, that you are in such trouble, but hope that you will come out of it, (perhaps a sadder, but still) a wiser man.

C

Chapter Third.

WHEN "Polished Sam" left home on this eventful morning, he had a smile on his lip, and a bright, gladsome look in his eye; and if he had the world before him, he had a bright and happy home behind him.

Believe me, good reader, that a bright and happy home is a wonderful back-up to a man, when he goes forth into a hard and cold world, to make his way through the day's business as best he can. On the present occasion, "Polished Sam" was backed up by Jenny, his wife; and by little Tommy, his son; and by Polly, the servant maid; they had all smiled him forth on his journey, and they would all smile him home again; aye, and Sam would be in a hurry to get home to all these smiling folk; and when he got a rub in the market from any of the " Rusty Joes" who might be there, he went famously through it all; for he knew he'd soon get home to peace, and quiet, and love again. You must not think, kind reader, that Sam Parsons didn't get knocks and rubs of all kinds in the world; he came in for his share; but he slipped through them better than other folk, for he was so civil and polished in his way; that, he disarmed the ill feeling of most.

The first person Sam Parsons came in sight of was old Biddy Magrath, the woman who sold apples at the corner of the street. " Good morning, Biddy," said Sam.

" Good morning, and good luck," answered Biddy; "is it to market ye's going to-day, Mr. Parsons?" (*Frontispiece.*)

"Yes, Biddy, can I do anything for you?" said Sam.

"Can ye do anything for me," answered Biddy, "to be sure ye can; bring me two ounces of the best tay, and half a pound of brown sugar, and here's the money;" and so saying, Biddy pulled forth a ball of rag from her pocket, which when unrolled, much after the fashion of an Egyptian mummy, developed a shilling.

"I'll get you a good cup," said Sam, as he took the shilling, "you'll never have a better cup than I wish you;" and he smacked his whip, and passed on.

Bridget Magrath had not much of the sunshine of the world falling upon her poor wrinkled face; and it was well for her she had naturally a cheerful temper; she led but a sorry life of it with the boys of the village; and Sam Parsons' kind word was one of the few gleams which fell to her lot. We can understand, therefore, the multitude of blessings wherewith Bridget overwhelmed Sam; how she called him all sorts of fine names; and at length, how she subsided behind her rickety table, to sell apples, if she could, all day long; but at any rate to wait for the evening, and Sam's arrival with the " tay."

No doubt, it was but a small kindness that Sam shewed, but he made a fellow-creature happy by it; in fact, he oiled old Biddy, as well as his wife, and child, and maid; and Bridget was not half so cross all that day, because she had the re-membrance of a kindly word and genial smile to help her through.

As Sam Parsons went to market, he had to surmount the same hill on which his neighbour " Rusty Joe " afterwards fared so badly; the road was just as steep, his horses' load was just as heavy; and nothing but a little oil carried him successfully up to the top. The wheels of Sam's waggon turned easily enough, for he had not neglected to grease them; but all the grease in the world could not make the wheels turn by themselves; it is true Sam had a little oil with him; (he generally had a little bottle amongst a few odds and ends in a box attached to his waggon) but one cannot oil horses' hoofs or joints; so, on the present occasion, unless Sam Parsons's were possessed of something more, he had little chance of surmounting Blackford hill; indeed, less chance than his neighbour "Rusty Joe" had after him, for his horses were not so strong. But Sam Parsons had another oil bottle, which was able effectually to do the work. Sam had a kind heart and word for man and beast; and this kind word carried him up. the Blackford hill; yes, he oiled his horses with it, and up they went. When first the team desired to stop, Sam let the poor beasts rest to recover breath; he put a couple of stones behind the waggon wheels, and then went round and patted each of the horses on

the neck; yes, he even rubbed their noses
with his hand; and the horses seemed to
understand that their master was caressing
and encouraging them. If human beings
rub noses in some part of the world, and
understand that form of salutation, why
should not man and beast understand each
other, when the former rubs the latter's
nose? Well! Sam Parsons rubbed his
horses' noses, and patted their necks, and
thus the cunning fellow oiled them well;
and when in a moment or two afterwards
he smacked his whip, just as a matter of
course, and cried "jee-hup," and made other
little persuasive noises, which we cannot
write down, for horse language is a thing
by itself; the team gave a pull, a long
pull, a strong pull, and a pull altogether,
and up the Blackford hill they went; and
not one of them required the lash.

Now, if Sam Parsons had told any one
that he oiled his horses at the Blackford
hill, he would in all probability have

been thought mad; nevertheless, dear reader, he did really oil them as much as he did the wheels of the waggon they drew; he oiled their tempers; and moreover, the oil put on them cost him nothing; and so the work was done. It is astonishing over what a surface a little oil will spread itself; astonishing, how many obstacles it will remove ; astonishing, how many evils it will avert. What a pity it is that folk don't know more of its value—kind words! kind deeds! kind looks! oh! they will often carry us up a hill of difficulty, where the lash, and oath, and angry temper, would prove of no avail.

The whole space of this little book would be absorbed, if we had to recount all Sam Parsons's ins and outs at the market town even this one day. Were we to undertake such a task, we should have to tell how "Polished Sam" was served with a specially nice bit at the market inn; for the waiter always had a kind word, and an "if you please," and a "thank you" from him, when he had little more than gruff orders from most of the other farmers. We should also have to relate how a dealer who thought Sam was very soft, because he was very civil, tried to " do " him in a bargain; but how our hero stood firm, for he was no fool, and did not want to be done, and got his fair price at last. We should also have to tell how Sam brought home a paper of sugar candy from the grocer, at whose shop he bought old Bridget's tea ; and how about a dozen folk, who were snarling and quarreling with each other, all had a smile for him. Furthermore, we should have to tell how our hero, by a few kind words, threw oil on the troubled waters, when he heard the naggling and snarling and jangling and general disagreeability which was going on between the barmaid and the head housemaid at the " Shock-of-Corn," the inn where Sam habitually put up.

Weren't these two feminines in a very nice frame of mind! Wasn't Mrs. Jullip's nose turned up in the air at Mrs. Duster?

and wasn't Mrs. Duster's turned down at Mrs. Jullip? and hadn't Mrs. Jullip said, "I would, in a minute!" and Mrs. Duster answered, "You would, would you;" and hadn't the one put her hands a-kimbo to stand upon her rights, and the other folded hers as much as to say, "I don't care a fig for them;" and if only they turned a little more round, wouldn't they have come to a regular bump; and who knows what? when our friend Sam in a masterly manner oiled them both; expressing his regret that two such long valued acquaintances should have had any misunderstanding, and his conviction that the whole thing must be an unfortunate mistake.

Under the judicious application of Sam's oiled feather, Mrs. Jullip's and Mrs. Duster's noses changed places; or rather, to speak more correctly, each met the other half way. Mrs. Jullip's nose, on being oiled, came a little down; and Mrs. Duster's, on experiencing the same process, went a little up; and, so, meeting as aforesaid, they both came right; and each looked her real old self again.

Believe me, Mrs. Duster's shoulder looked much more elegant when she dropped it to its proper slope, than when she tilted it up in the air like the back, and indeed, for the matter of that, the point of the tail of the " Shock-of-Corn's " black cat; a dreadfully quarrelsome creature, which said, " Phit, phit, hiss, meaow, phit, phiz," and we had almost said, " bang, bang," on even the smallest provocation; when any cat, in a proper frame of mind, would have seen with half an eye, that such a display of phits and phizes and energy, was wholly uncalled for and out of place.

But why say, good reader, how much we *could* tell you, when we don't mean to do anything of the kind, and when it is high time for " Polished Sam " to be thinking of going home.

Chapter Fourth.

"RUSTY JOE" made a bad day's business of it: he never got to market at all. A little examination of the harness showed that it was completely done for; and he had to untackle his horses; leave his waggon there; and make the best of his way home. With one delay and another, it was coming on evening before this unfortunate man could fetch his waggon home again. "Rusty Joe" tried one person and another in the village who had harness; he sent to some of his brother farmers round about, but no one seemed inclined to go out of his way to oblige him; they had all, at some time, met with rudeness at his hands; and now, they did not want to have anything to do with him. Of course, we are not commending their conduct; they ought to have returned good for evil; but, as is too often the case, they did not.

So much time was consumed in sending about to the neighbours, and in endeavouring to cobble up a harness of rope that, it was coming on evening, before " Rusty Joe " was able to return with his horses to the waggon; and when he reached it, he was destined to meet with a fresh trouble—the waggon was not as he had left it; the covering had evidently been moved; and poor Joe found out, only too soon, the reason why; for no small part of the contents of the waggon . had been stolen; a gipsy party had passed that way, and they had made free with the unguarded property.

When "Rusty Joe" found that he had not only lost his market, but also some of the produce that he was carrying there;

and when he reflected that it was upon
the sale of that very produce he was in
part depending to pay his rent, he became
as savage as an old bear; he cursed and
swore; but that, like all cursing and swear-
ing, did him no good; and at last he sat
down by the roadside. "Rusty Joe" had not
been there many minutes, when he heard
the sound of wheels; and soon "Polished
Sam" appeared in sight, with his team;
Sam was whistling like a blackbird, and the
bells on his horses were tinkling cheerily;
and he and the team seemed more like
a merry family party than anything else.
A moment's glance was sufficient to show
Sam Parsons that there was something
wrong, and he hastened as fast as he safely
could, down the hill, to meet his unhappy
neighbour; to sympathize, and help. But
"Rusty Joe," wanted no help; no, not
he! "some folk were lucky, and some were
unlucky: and he didn't want other folk
to be prying into, and meddling with, his

affairs;" and the ungracious man carried on
in this style for full half an hour. As Joe
would not be helped, of course Sam could
not interfere; but he found various excuses
for dawdling about, until his neighbour had
managed to get the horses harnessed and
put to; then, with a muttered curse or two,
the man and his horses started for home.
But oh! what a chorus of creaks came
from his dry and squeaking wheels; and so
stiffly and heavily did the waggon roll, that
there is no knowing when it would have
reached home, or whether it would not have
broken down again by the way, had not
Sam Parsons ventured to offer a little help
once more. Sam, in the kindness of his
heart, had kept close to his neighbour;
and now he made bold to suggest that the
waggon could never be got home without
a little grease; "You heard it creaking,
neighbour," said he to "Rusty Joe;" "and
I believe it was just for want of a little
grease, it stuck so fast upon the hill;"

so saying, Sam Parsons produced a little from his waggon, and managed to get it well on to the creaking wheels. Marvellous was the change! the creaks suddenly subsided into silence and the horses easily drew their load; even the patched-up harness was quite equal to its work, so slight was the strain put upon it.

With all his grumpy tempers, "Rusty Joe" was not sorry to receive such substantial help; so he allowed Sam Parsons to walk by his side, Sam's waggon following close behind. Sam was not long before he spied Joe halting very much on one foot— he sympathized with him for having corns, and had just begun a dissertation on the virtue of a certain corn plaister; when his companion told him that it was stiff shoe leather that was doing the mischief; "the boots are as stiff as if they were frozen," said "Rusty Joe," "ever since the last market day, when they got such a wetting." "Whee-o-," whistled Sam, "I'll soften them in two minutes;" and slipping behind to his waggon, he brought forth his oil bottle, and gave the boots a good anointing with its contents. Of course the cure could not be perfect in so short a time; still "Rusty Joe" could not but see that a little oil was able to do wonders; the boots seemed to have become quite good-natured; and it was a question whether a little more oil would not make them even frolicksome; "I have great faith in oil," said Sam Parsons, "I oil almost everything; this very morning I oiled the lock of my street door, and my penknife, and I greased my waggon wheels, and I oiled my wife, and child, and I gave the servant maid a touch too; and I tell you what it is, neighbour Joe, I slip along famously, where I find many another sticks fast." "Rusty Joe's" torn nail seemed to give him a fresh twinge, when the penknife was spoken about; and as to the wife! his conscience reminded him how bearishly he had behaved to her at breakfast. "What do you mean by oiling your wife, man," said "Rusty Joe," rather tartly; "you haven't been sneaky have you, and knocking under to a woman?" and "Rusty Joe" edged away from "Polished Sam's" sides, as though he were near some slimy serpent. "No indeed," answered Sam, "I've not been knocking any way, neither over nor under; but I just gave her and the bantling a loving word before I started from home; and I said a kind word to the lass to cheer her up through her work for the day; and for the matter of that, I gave the old apple woman a touch of my oiled feather too: few people say a kind word to her, and so I did; and I dare say, it helped her through the day too!" "I wouldn't cringe to any one living," continued "Polished Sam," "not to the Queen herself; but to cringe is one thing, to be civil, respectful, and loving, according as the case requires, is another; I never knew ill come of it, and I've often known good. Yes, neighbour, I've known the good of it in my own house, over and over again—there's my Jenny, you don't know the work there's in that little creature; bless you! she'd work herself to the finger bone, if you give her a kind word; I knowed her to sit up seven nights with me, without taking off a stitch of her clothes, that time I broke my leg; and when I said to her one morning, as the day was breaking, and I looked at her red eyelids, 'Jenny, my darling, I can never pay you for all this'— didn't she laugh and say, 'why, Sam, how can you tell such a story, you've paid me now?'"

"Paid you, woman; why, what do you mean?"

"Didn't you say *my darling?*"

"To be sure I did," said Sam.

"Well! wasn't that payment *to a woman's heart?*"

"And she looked so earnest like at me, that I felt the tears come into my eyes;—

Oh, neighbour, I couldn't say it as she said it; for these women have a way of speaking that don't belong to us men; sometimes I think there's something that makes music in their throats; but ever since that day, I've been ten times as loving as I was before; and I try to say a kind word, not only to Jenny, but to every one I meet. I believe, neighbour," continued Sam, " that women's of that nature that they'll do anything for love—no use our driving them, our scolding, and ordering, and banging about; that only makes slaves of them; but give them a little love, and they'll do wonders." As Sam Parsons found that his neighbour was listening, he was encouraged to go on, even though he received no answer. " And I do the same," said Sam, " by every wench that comes to service to me ; servants are made of the same stuff as their mistresses ; they all have hearts, and the same kind of oil will reach them all."

Thus discoursing, Sam Parsons arrived at

his own farm yard; there was Jenny his
wife ready to meet him with a kiss, and
there was Tommy, who received his father
with a " click, click," leaving it a matter of
speculation as to whether he had not been
clicking ever since the morning until now;
and then there was Polly the servant maid

standing close to the irons, which shone as though they were fresh from the shop; she hoped they'd catch her master's eye, and she knew she'd get a kind word; and when Sam went into the sitting room, there he saw a great heap of his stockings which Jenny had been darning; and when Sam sat down to tea, there was a pie that Jenny had made; and if Sam had been a little boy instead of a grown-up man, he would certainly have patted his chest and smacked his lips, and so expressed his opinion that, that was "something like a pie." One would think that Sam Parsons had oiled the pie, so smoothly did each piece slip down his throat, for he was at peace with Jenny his wife, Tommy his son, and Polly the servant maid. Good humour promotes digestion, and our readers will be glad to hear that Sam slept well upon that good supper, and had pleasant dreams; his only nightmare being that, he pursued an eccentric cock in vain; which not appreciating the honor intended for him, viz., that he should contribute a portion of his tail for a feather for Mr. Parsons' oil flask, and so possibly lose some of his charms in the eyes of his seven wives, made off with himself, in a head-long and ridiculous and altogether undignified kind of way, as quick as his legs could carry him.   And Mr. Parsons woke up refreshed, to be happy, and make others happy all day long.

Chapter Fifth.

OUR friend "Rusty Joe" shall have the last chapter all to himself. And first of all it must be told that, "Polished Sam's" observations were not altogether thrown away upon him. Although he wouldn't let on to other folk that he was a miserable man; still he really was so, and he owned it to himself; his conscience kept saying to him " you are all of a piece, 'force, force,' 'must, must,' 'shall, shall,' for everybody and everything." The contrast between his happy neighbour and his miserable self could not but strike the poor man's mind; and he made a desperate resolution to reform.

"I'll do it, I'll do it," said Joe in a loud voice; never thinking that there was any one to hear him; but it so happened that the parson was close behind; and struck with his parishioner's energy, he said, "Do what?" "Reform," answered Joe, like a man in a dream, who felt himself obliged to speak whether he liked or not.

"We can't reform in anything without the grace of God to help us," said the minister; "and we must ask for that, Mr. Irons."

This speech seemed to rouse Joe up, and he felt very queer, when he found himself actually embarked in a conversation with the parson—all this was so very new, that Joe didn't quite like it; and indeed he would have backed out of the conversation as quickly as possible, but that the parson who always stuck like a piece of wax to his work, was too glad to get a word with his rusty parishioner, easily to let him go. Gently and gradually he drew from the poor crest-fallen fellow the whole of what was in his mind; and when Joe came to his own house, he even asked the parson in.

The minister felt like a fish out of water in Joe Irons' house; but it was very well that he went in; for Joe's wife, irritated by the destruction of her solitary ornament, and by her husband's rude way of speaking, had not done his shirt, nor paid any very special attention to what he was to eat. The minister's presence prevented any harsh words; and his wise and loving counsel led Joe and his wife to forgive and forget the past and commence afresh that night, by asking for strength from heaven to speak, do, and be like Jesus Christ. He read for them that night the 133rd Psalm, and shewed them "how good and pleasant it is for brethren to dwell together in unity; how it is like the precious ointment upon the head that ran down upon the beard, even Aaron's beard, that went down to the skirts of his garment; as the dew of Hermon, and as the dew that descended

on the mountains of Zion, for there the
Lord commanded the blessing, even life
for evermore."

That very night Joe began. When the
minister was going, he actually handed him
his hat, and made a kind of attempt at
a bow at the door; and Joe's wife began,
for she bathed his poor broken nail, and
sat up nearly all night to get ready his
shirt; and when the morning came, "Rusty
Joe" oiled almost everything he had; and
in a twelve months' time, he was liked as
well as any one in the parish. Yes! there
were no more bangings of doors in Joe
Irons' house; there were no more rough
words between him and his wife; there was
enough of kindness to make home com-
fortable, and a little to spare to make
neighbours agreeable, and Joe Irons became a happy man. Joe's choicest friend
was henceforth "Polished Sam;" and Joe
kept as close to his skirts as though he
expected to rub some of the polish from

him upon himself. Joe never forgot the
parson's advice to seek strength for improve-
ment on his knees; and by way of a

reminder, that he should not forget his new
principles, he hung something over his
bedroom mantlepiece, so that it should be

the first thing that met his eyes when he awoke; and what do you think it was, good reader? there it is in the picture:—

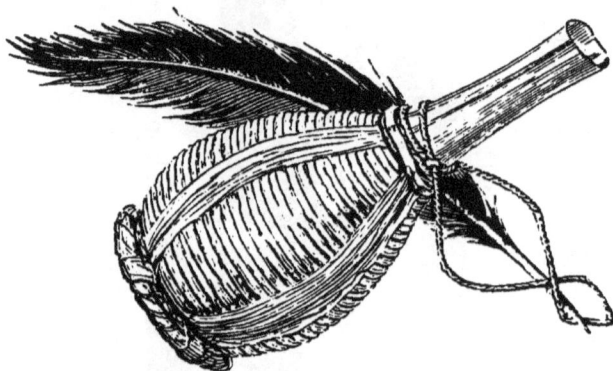

THE OILED FEATHER.

FLETCHER AND SON, PRINTERS, NORWICH.

www.ingramcontent.com/pod-product-compliance
Lightning Source LLC
Chambersburg PA
CBHW022029080426
42733CB00007B/778